Phonics Things
sounds, vocabulary, poetry, & art

Written by Brian Kissman

Illustrations by Brian Kissman
with Wendy Simons

Poetry by Brian Kissman,
with Eric Nilsson and Carol Kaplan

www.learnonpoint.com

An OnPoint Original
Phonics Things
sounds, vocabulary, poetry & art
By Brian Kissman

Copyright © 2007, 2015 by Kissman Educational Consulting and Publishing, Inc.

Illustrations by Brian Kissman and Wendy Simons
Poetry by Brian Kissman, Eric Nilsson, and Carol Kaplan
Graphic Design by Ethan Kaplan

ISBN: 978-0-9798172-0-5   Second Edition

PT-11-2015-RD

Acknowledgements

Special thanks to family, friends, and colleagues for their support throughout the evolution of Phonics Things.

And with appreciation to writers, artists, and musicians who confirm my passion for creating something out of nothing.

www.learnonpoint.com

Sales & Distribution

LearnOnPoint
15300 Red Arrow Highway
Union Pier, MI 49129
Email: info@learnonpoint.com
Web: www.learnonpoint.com

table of contents

introduction

Why This Book?
Phonics Things is an ABC book for the 21st Century.

The Problem: The Achievement Gap
One of the biggest problems in education is a child arriving to school unprepared to learn to read. Research shows that up to 70% of 8th graders and 65% of 12th graders read below grade level. But, research also shows that these students arrive to school without the foundation to learn to read and consequently struggle to catch up throughout their school years despite the best efforts of our schools.

Education starts at home. But in our busy modern world, too many parents don't find the time or have the tools and skills to help their children build a foundation for reading. Missing these opportunities in the early developmental years causes learning delays that can stretch well into a child's school years and even into adulthood.

This is the achievement gap; the difference between the kids who arrive at school with solid foundations for learning to read and those that do not. Though most all students will progress academically, the gap too often remains. However, we can close the achievement gap if we know what to do and that is what makes Phonics Things revolutionary. It builds the school to home partnership by providing a common language with shared understandings to grow phonemic awareness, phonics, reading fluency, vocabulary, and reading comprehension.

A Solution: Closing the Achievement Gap
To close the achievement gap, we first must grow phonemic awareness; we intentionally expose the learner to the sounds of the English language so that they are ready to learn to develop proficiency with phonics and reading fluency in elementary school. Phonics Things does this and much more. This entertaining learning tool provides us the foundation to learn to read. It serves young children entering pre-school, elementary students, and it also fills the void for struggling readers who need remediation. And, Phonics Things is highly effective for those learning English as a second language. With Phonics Things we gain phonemic awareness and the phonics skills necessary to develop reading fluency, which is a prerequisite to develop reading comprehension.

Phonics Things features the sounds of the English language. We learn these sounds through colorful paintings that serve as indelible illustrations and zany poems that present a rich diversity of vocabulary. Word lists present learners with academic vocabulary in language arts, social studies, science, and math. Whether exposing little ones to the sounds of the English language to grow phonemic awareness or helping older ones learn phonics through word study, Phonics Things makes learning fun.

Phonics Things educates us in entertaining ways. With Phonics Things, we experience the sounds of the English language, learn to sound out and syllabicate words, read with fluency, expand vocabulary, develop comprehension skills, and build an appreciation for art and culture.

How to Use This Book

With the little ones, the aim is all about exposure to the sounds of the English language and growing phonemic awareness, rather than learning the sounds or words. That said, if a child is an early bloomer and ready to learn, then we differentiate accordingly.

For the older ones, the aim is to grow proficiency with phonics, reading fluency, vocabulary, and comprehension.

Learning to read with Phonics Things, use the following strategies:

- Think aloud about the word and its illustration. Sound out the illustrated word with taps or claps.
- Engage in conversation to create a story to go with the illustration.
- Read aloud, think aloud, and engage in conversation about the definition and figurative language sample.
- Read aloud the poem with fluency, expression, and pace.
- Engage in echo and oral choral readings.
- Retell or summarize the poem's story or ideas.
- Make connections, generate questions, and make inferences about the poem's story or ideas.
- Engage in conversation about a word to grow awareness of the word's meaning.
- Grow phonemic awareness of the sounds within words. With tap or clap blending, sound out one syllable words and syllabicate multi-syllable words.
- Use each word from the list in a sentence. Engage in conversation about the meaning of the word in the context of the sentence.
- Perform the poems and develop the Traits of Presentation (volume, clarity, fluency, expression, pace, body language, and eye contact).
- Develop phonemic awareness, phonics, reading fluency, vocabulary, and comprehension with the Section 6 rules, lists, and strategies.
- Working with the 10 lists of 100 sight words, write 5 sentences a day, a sentence for each word.
- Write a poem for each illustration.

Never underestimate a child's or learner's ability to decipher the English language on their own. Phonics Things makes it easy to do.

Phonics Things is an enjoyable experience in sight and sound.

When it comes to literacy and lifelong learning, it starts with the ABCs!

Brian Kissman, Author and Educator

the english alphabet

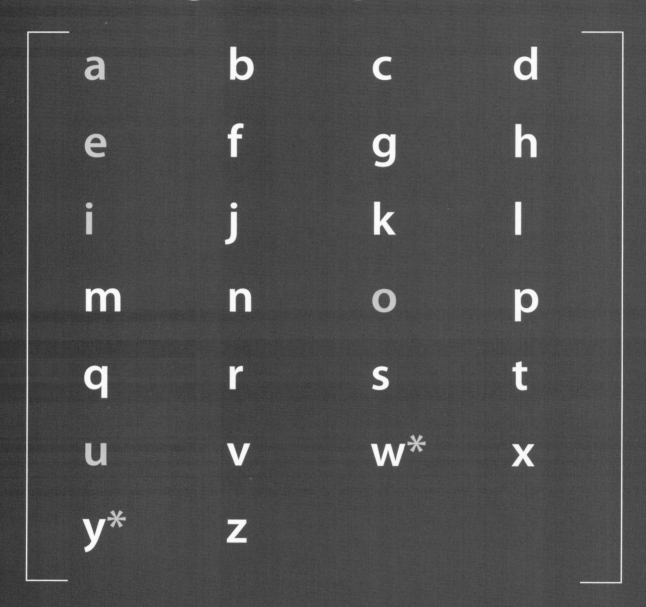

a   b   c   d

e   f   g   h

i   j   k   l

m   n   o   p

q   r   s   t

u   v   w*   x

y*   z

5 vowel letters
+ 21 consonant letters
26 letters in all

*The consonant y sometimes acts as a vowel by making the long e sound or the long i sound.
*The consonant w sometimes acts as a vowel when it is next to an a, e, or o.

1.
letters of the english alphabet

definition > a hard round red, yellow or green fruit that is white inside and has a crisp, sweet taste

idiom > Marwan is the apple of my eye. (one who is treasured)

apple

We slip slices of crispy apple
into grandma's famous pie.
Our family bakes together
to honor the Fourth of July.

Eating apple pie with ice cream
is a delicious, dandy delight.
It's a treat we'll share together
while watching fireworks tonight.

Sweets and flags and grand displays
make it a special time of year.
It's our nation's annual birthday;
cherish the freedom we hold dear!

application
agriculture
antonym

analyze
stamp
past

mass
latin
calendar

definition > a door, usually on hinges, in a fence or outside wall

analogy > Gate is to fence as hatch is to submarine.

gate

Through the gleaming, glittering gate,
past a luscious green backyard,
I happily bounce along the path
with Brandon's birthday card.

A sweet surprise is planned for him,
and, if he only knew!
All his friends are hiding here,
but he doesn't have a clue.

We've come for Brandon's special day;
it's time to celebrate.
Hurray! The games that we will play
will make this party great.

a

ate
Asia
acre

pace
May
female

courageous
Monday
sundae

definition > a large motor vehicle that carries passengers

simile > The football player was built like a bus.

bus

This bus, so big and bright and new,
will take us on a tour
to see the desert mountains,
so bountiful and pure.

Cruising through the valley,
we truly are amazed,
beautiful flowering cacti,
sparse fields where livestock graze.

This amazing adventuresome trip
was planned so we would have the chance
to smell the arid air
and watch majestic horses prance!

b

boy
billion
bibliography

obscure
obey
abdomen

hubbub
corncob
crab

definition > an electronic machine that stores information and uses programs to help find, change, or organize the information

alliteration > Carla concluded the computer is a critical tool for computation and communication.

computer

The computer burps and beeps and yawns,
commanding operations.
How very smart it seems to be,
making calculations.

We travel to the Internet,
superhighway of a sort.
We communicate with data there,
and fly from port to port.

Websites are engaging places
full of information.
Computers are used around the world
for work and recreation.

C

could
couldn't
could've

picture
second
American

Atlantic
Pacific
semantic

definition > an instrument, used for writing or drawing, made of wood with a graphite or colored center, that typically has an eraser at one end

simile > Bibi was as thin as a pencil.

pencil

My pencil is sharp, not shoddy,
to help keep my writing neat.
The secret of some poems, you know,
is to make them short and sweet!

The first step is to think a lot
about what I want to say;
then I construct an outline
to guide me on my way.

I draft, revise, and publish it,
then communicate my piece.
In the end I present my poem,
inspired by Matisse!

C

city
circle
cylinder

concert
percent
peaceful

face
since
dance

17

definition > a very common animal with four legs and fur that is typically kept as a pet or used to guard buildings

alliteration > The dogs dawdled and danced in the dark.

dogs

The fleabags drift so freely.
They roam throughout the park.
They run and jump and dance around,
and never leave till dark.

The pack, it croodles and dawdles
in playful games of chase.
Each dog is craggy and shaggy.
Each has its own cute face.

We watch with blinking eyes
as they race across the field.
Zipping through nooks and crannies,
they'll never be well-healed.

d

dessert
desert
discover

e**d**it
a**dd**ition
deca**d**e

ol**d**
en**d**
blen**d**

19

egg

definition > an oval object with a hard shell that contains yolk

idiom > Kareem put all his eggs in one basket. (to risk everything on a single venture)

egg

Peering through the incubator
believing not our eyes,
we knew a lizard would soon emerge,
a wicked, winning prize.

The moment had arrived!
An egg began to hatch.
A tiny reptile was creeping out,
the first one of the batch.

The terrarium is waiting;
'twas prepared with gentle care.
We'll catch the lizard by its tail
and relocate it there!

energy
estimation
ebony

elephant
n**e**xt
sent**e**nce

s**e**gment
c**e**ntury
d**e**cimeter

definition > a long thin fish with sharp teeth that looks like a snake

analogy > Eel is to lair as bird is to nest.

eel

A snakelike, scaleless fish,
the Moray eel's a fearsome sight.
When diving, don't get close
unless you're looking for a fight!

This beast with a greedy nature
is hiding in its lair,
waiting to catch a dainty fish
to ravage without care.

It strikes like bright white lightening;
it's over in a blink!
This underwater predator
leaves nothing left to sink!

east
electricity
evaluate

week
meter
Venus

December
receive
receipt

definition > one of the light soft structures covering the body of a bird

idiom > Getting this position would certainly be a feather in Mai's cap.
(an act or deed to one's credit, a distinctive achievement)

feather

A fine and light, flat feather
with a long and hollow shaft,
he used this pointed crimson quill
to write his final draft.

The author plucked this age-old pen
from a fast and feathered bird.
He wrote at night by candlelight;
the breezes never stirred.

Hungrily I consumed the book;
I journeyed through the text.
I read and wondered how and why,
and what would happen next?

f

fact
fiction
February

affect
effect
nonfiction

off
stiff
wolf

25

definition > a game, played outdoors on a course, the object being to hit a small white ball with a club into a series of 18 holes, using as few hits as possible to win

alliteration > The grand game of golf is played on green grass.

golf

Golf is a glorious game
played on an outdoor course.
You swing the club and try to aim
with great, triumphant force.

Most people play just for fun,
though some folks play as pros.
The competition can be tough
as they battle nose-to-nose.

An eagle or a birdie
are both impressive scores,
but even if you bogey,
for beginners – not too poor!

g

gold
gallon
goals

sugar
fragment
diagonal

gardening
gargling
analog

definition > any precious stone that is cut into a particular shape for jewelry

simile > Lalana sparkled like a gem.

gem

A large and precious gem
of beauty and perfection,
he gave his love a ring,
a sign of his affection.

It sparkles bright and pure,
a gorgeous stone quite rare.
You ask, "Can he afford it?"
Why yes! He's a millionaire!

A treasured jewel it is,
a rare stone prized by many;
but if she loves him not,
then it isn't worth a penny!

g

giant
genre
geology

digit
gorgeous
imagine

village
huge
bridge

definition > a piece of cloth that you wear on your head for fashion or protection from weather

metaphor > Texas Tim's cowboy hat was a crown in the eyes of the townsfolk.

hat

A handsome cowboy hat,
of rich brown, hand-hewn leather,
is cut and stitched to tolerate
the very toughest weather.

Each and every ranch hand,
hired year-by-year,
is gifted with a cowboy hat.
It's quite a souvenir!

A wrangler wears it with honor
each time he goes to town,
he brushes off the hay and dust
from his hallowed cowboy crown.

h

hundred
hundredth
horizontal

a**h**ead
a**h**oy
be**h**ind

be**h**oove
re**h**earsal
over**h**eard

31

definition > a dome-like shelter made from blocks of hard snow and ice packed together

metaphor > The igloo was a bubble on the horizon.

igloo

Just beyond the snowdrift,
past the soaring white curlew,
sits a dome-shaped dwelling,
a glittering, glazed igloo.

Built with blocks and bits of snow,
and shaped with whittled care,
this solid Northern shelter shines
with sparkling frozen flair.

Air-tight, safe protection
in frigid, Arctic winds,
it's here that we'll take refuge
before the storm begins.

i

ill
important
interpret

visualize
kilometer
scribble

infinite
until
unit

definition > a vehicle with two wheels, a seat, and handle bars that you ride by pushing pedals with your feet

analogy > Bicycle is to Tour de France as horse is to Kentucky Derby.

b**i**cycle

A drafty way to travel
on two slick, shiny wheels,
with cushy seat and handlebars,
I like the way it feels!

This is my bright blue touring bike,
fit and ready for the road.
The journey is well-planned, you see;
there's food and water stowed.

I'm cruising Lakeshore Drive
as it winds along the Bay.
The breeze is blowing through my hair;
I bet I could bike all day!

ivory
ice
icicle

cl**i**mate
d**i**alogue
tr**i**angle

d**i**nosaur
f**i**nite
incl**i**ne

definition >   a type of motor vehicle with all-wheel drive made for travel
over rough terrain (trademark)

personification >   The jeep attacked the steep mountain with ease.

jeep

Through mountainous, lush green jungles
our safari jeep will roll.
When shielding threatened animals,
we're always on patrol.

Tigers are our animal friends,
endangered more than most.
Let's team up to protect them
from coast to coast to coast.

More people and less land
are challenges we face.
We all must work together
with gentle, loving grace.

January
June
July

object
rejoice
subject

overjoyed
adjective
majority

definition > a toy, made from a light frame covered in paper or plastic, that you fly in the wind at the end of a long string

hyperbole > Kumar's kite was so high it touched the clouds.

kite

A kite of red and orange,
a geometric design,
Mike bought it at the hobby shop
along with tough, fine twine.

One sunny day in May,
the wind was feeling right.
In just no time at all,
Mike's kite reached height in flight!

Flown with consummate skill,
over and up and down,
it soared and roared high in the sky,
grinning down upon the town!

kilometer
kangaroo
kindergarten

token
market
turkey

kayak
schoolwork
think

definition > a glass object, with a filament, that is screwed into a lamp and produces light

analogy > Light bulb is to lamp as flame is to candle.

light bulb

Gently flick the switch
and a light bulb burns so bright,
glowing in dark places,
making sunshine in the night.

Edison was the inventor.
He knew what we would need;
even when the day grew dim,
we'd want to play and read.

When I'm too scared to fall asleep,
I turn my night light on.
Presto! There's a gleam of light;
and all the ghosts are gone!

I

latitude
longitude
language

illustrator
illustration
milliliter

parallel
powerful
swell

definition > a box, usually outside a house, where letters are delivered or collected

personification > The mailbox stood tall and proud near the front gate.

mailbox

To mail my precious entry,
I raised the red, metal flag.
I placed my work in the mailbox;
then time began to drag.

As always, the postman came early
at dawn on the very next day.
He reached and pulled the parcel out.
Whoosh! He took my essay away!

The contest rules were explicit,
"…due by the first day of September."
Yes! My story would win a prize
with words they were sure to remember.

m

minute
moderation
molecular

comma
symmetry
diameter

medium
maximum
kilogram

definition > a thin, pointed piece of metal with a flat end that you pound into a piece of wood or material, using a hammer

idiom > Nanako nailed the test on her first try. (to be wildly successful)

nail

You could call them oversized pins,
hammered to get the job done.
Nails keep things neatly in place,
pounded down one-by-one.

Solid for hundreds of years,
used in functional ways,
crafted of muscular metal,
they refuse to go down in decay!

When crafting things made of wood,
these iron sticks do the job.
Yes they will, they most certainly will,
help form a thing-a-ma-bob.

n

numerator
north
November

denominator
answer
patience

nation
paragon
octagon

definition > a long cylinder-shaped piece of cooked meat eaten in a bun

idiom > Remy was a hot dog on the basketball court.
(showing your best; show-off)

46

hot dog

Spicy and juicy hot dogs
are a moveable feast, you see.
The hot dog fits exceedingly well
in a roll with a center crease.

You find them at the ball park;
you can hear the vendor holler.
He fills his lungs and yells, "Hot Dog!"
and charges a couple of dollars.

Mustard and ketchup and relish
are the typical hot dog trimmings.
It's hard for me to eat just one,
I'm hoping for extra innings!

odd
October
opportunity

problem
copy
follow

modern
pottery
raindrop

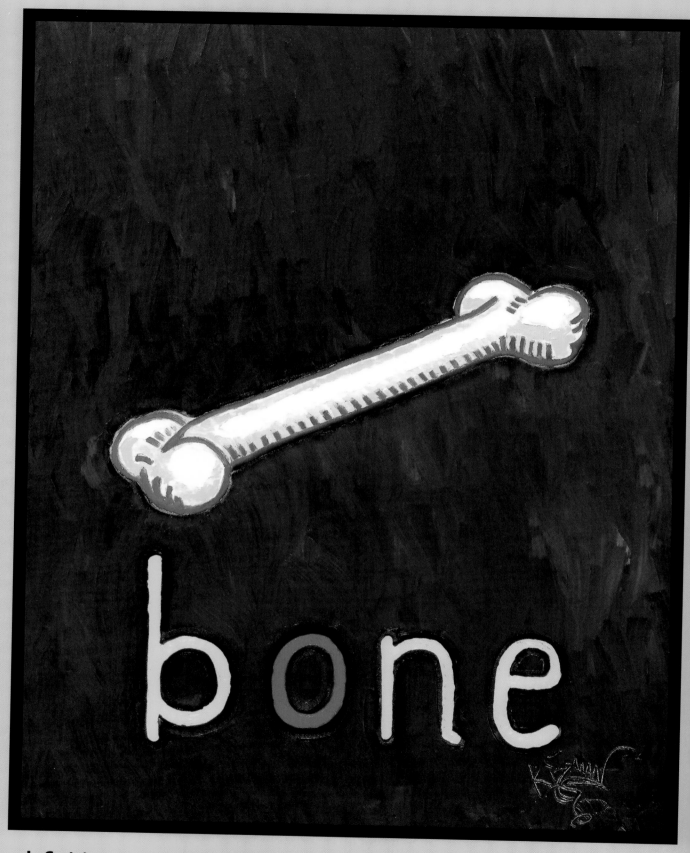

definition >   one of the hard pieces of the skeleton of a human or animal body

idiom >   Barbara had a bone to pick with her friend. (a complaint)

bone

Furry Fido pranced to my feet
as I talked to my friend on the phone.
There, he begged for his favorite treat;
so I tossed him a flavorable bone.

He slobbered all over his snack,
then carried it quickly away.
He gnawed with a burning desire,
as he chewed, he showed little delay.

He snuggled up comfy and cozy
in his bed near the warm fireplace.
Sated, elated, though that bone's overrated,
he's at peace in his usual space.

oval
open
ocean

n**o**tes
mel**o**dy
telesc**o**pe

hell**o**
zer**o**
pian**o**

definition > an instrument made of plastic or metal used for writing and drawing in ink

alliteration > Penelope punctuated her paper perfectly using a plastic pen.

pen

I pondered my pointy ink pen,
to see how it was made.
A simple idea – a brilliant idea –
thoughts can get out, be written, conveyed.

A ball point invented for writing,
its blue ink rolls perfectly well.
A fancy and blue-blended casing
makes it attractive and easy to sell.

Designed and crafted with care,
imported from far, far away,
it's used to write notes and letters,
a story, a poem or a play!

p

poetry
pyramid
pentagon

preposition
computer
composition

Europe
map
group

51

definition > a female ruler of a country, either from a royal family or the wife of a king

alliteration > King Quincy was quick to quibble with his quiet queen.

queen

The quintessential queen
was a noble wife to the king,
esteemed and respected by all,
for the special songs she would sing.

She brought us to the square
in the early afternoons;
we watched the jester dancing
to her quirky, perky tunes.

With a zest for life and living,
she embraced her royal role.
Kindness, love and compassion
were etched on her heart and soul.

q

quart
quote
quotation

inquire
liquid
sequence

earthquake
equation
equivalent

definition > a tool used for removing dead leaves from areas of grass or to make soil level

idiom > It was not right that he was raked over the coals for his mistake.
(to reprimand severely)

rake

Hear the crunch of the freshly-raked leaves
on a clear and crisp autumn day,
beneath a cloudless blue sky,
we were getting ready to play.

While our parents made jumpable piles,
we danced near the barnyard door.
When the piles had grown as high as the moon,
we shouted, "We want more!"

When all the heaps were completed,
my cousin yelled, "Ready, set, go!"
We leaped in feet first with an energy burst,
while the grown-ups all hollered, "Whoa!"

r

resolution
relationship
ratio

around
deride
Uranus

correction
irrigation
interruption

definition > a tool made for cutting material, such as paper or cloth, consisting of two sharp blades fastened together with handles for your finger and thumb

simile > Juanito cut through the work like scissors through paper.

scissors

Scissors can be a dangerous tool
with sleek and slippery blades.
As long as you're crafty and careful,
there will be no need for first aid.

A great idea pops into my head,
my hand on paper, my fingers fanned!
I trace around them, cut them out.
It goes as I had planned!

I keep cutting and collaging,
having tons of fabulous fun.
Scissoring here and pasting there,
a masterpiece is begun!

S

Saturday
Sunday
setting

synthesize
question
possessive

Mars
lyrics
continents

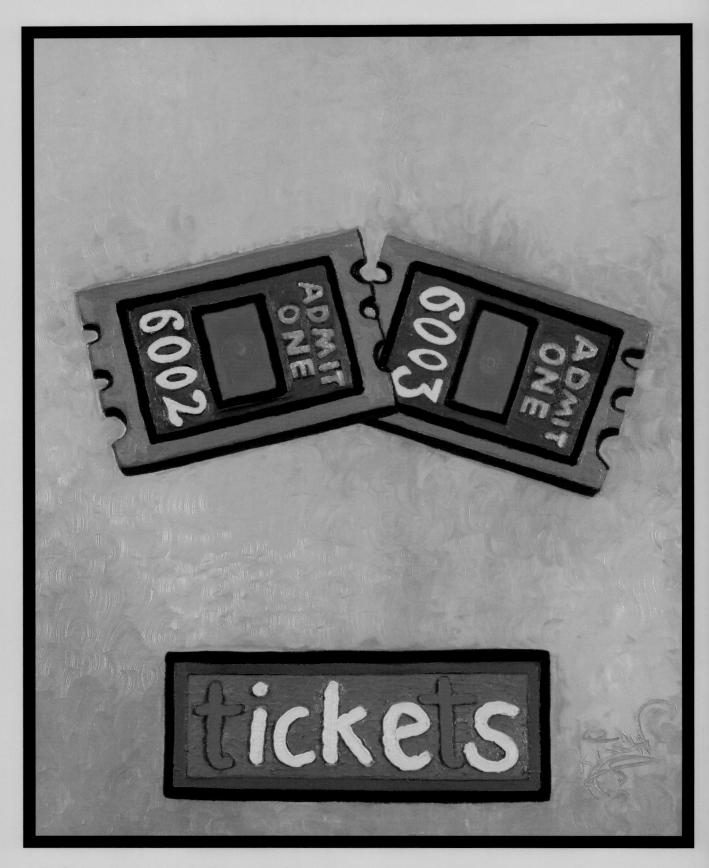

definition > printed pieces of paper that show that you have paid to do something

idiom > Tamara's talent is her ticket to success. (a key factor)

tickets

I had a couple of tickets
to the cage-free Zulu Zoo.
One was for my admission,
the other – for Max – made two.

We spotted the wild monkeys
in trees that touched the sky;
and beneath our feet, deep in the grass,
great pythons slithered by!

For a trendy, transporting adventure,
please come to this wonderful land.
You'll dive with dolphins in the sea
and dig with the turtles in sand!

top
today
tomorrow

pa**tt**ern
con**t**en**t**
yes**t**erday

con**t**act
par**t**
summi**t**

definition > a round arc-shaped object that you hold above your head to protect yourself from the rain or sun

metaphor > Nizhoni was protected by an umbrella of love.

umbrella

A water-proof, circular canopy
protects us from sun and rain.
The umbrella, simply a handy thing,
this one is red and plain!

Mounted high on a metal rod,
it's easy to learn to use,
a very fun thing to open and close,
and an easy thing to lose!

Amy was strolling down the street,
when it began to pour.
Zip! Her umbrella shot right up,
and kept her dry to her front door.

under
unimportant
umpire

p**u**blish
s**u**mmarize
s**u**btraction

halib**u**t
omnib**u**s
Celsi**u**s

unicorn

definition > an imaginary animal that looks like a white horse with a special horn on its forehead

analogy > Unicorn is to fantasy as horse is to reality.

unicorn

The unbelievable unicorn
gallops at an amazing pace.
A moonlit sky and stardust eyes
enhance its elegant grace.

It's a mighty, magical creature,
so fanciful, friendly and free.
Imagine it prancing and dancing;
what an awesome dream to see!

We visualize it in our minds,
the mythical unicorn!
A creature of wonder, a fantasy,
oh, I wish that one could be born!

u

useless
universe
usual

volume
pollution
execute

destitute
menu
emu

van

definition > a box-like motor vehicle with back or side doors, used for transporting people or carrying goods

simile > The moving van was as big as Liam's house.

van

The delivery van veered towards our house;
our equipment was finally here.
For three long, ponderous weeks,
we'd been waiting for our gear.

Now we finally have the tools
to climb the sheer rock face,
to scale a lofty mountain side,
to forge a challenging race!

Climbing rocks can be very tricky;
we do our best to prepare.
Using our tools, we scramble up high,
from the top we can see everywhere!

vertical

vegetable

value

revise

revive

conventions

believe

wave

solve

definition > a small cart with four wheels and a handle in the front, used as a toy for children

alliteration > Wally wheeled the wagon down the wide, winding path.

66

wagon

A simple spoke-wheeled wagon,
it's such a super cool cart.
Its playful design and color
made it a great work of art.

We use it to carry and pull things.
We create a world of new games.
It can change and morph in a second;
it never remains the same.

One day it's grand as a chariot;
the next day it glides like a plane.
Our countless wild and woolly adventures
are always new and never the same!

W

west
Wednesday
water

unwind
aware
outward

mugwump
forward
backward

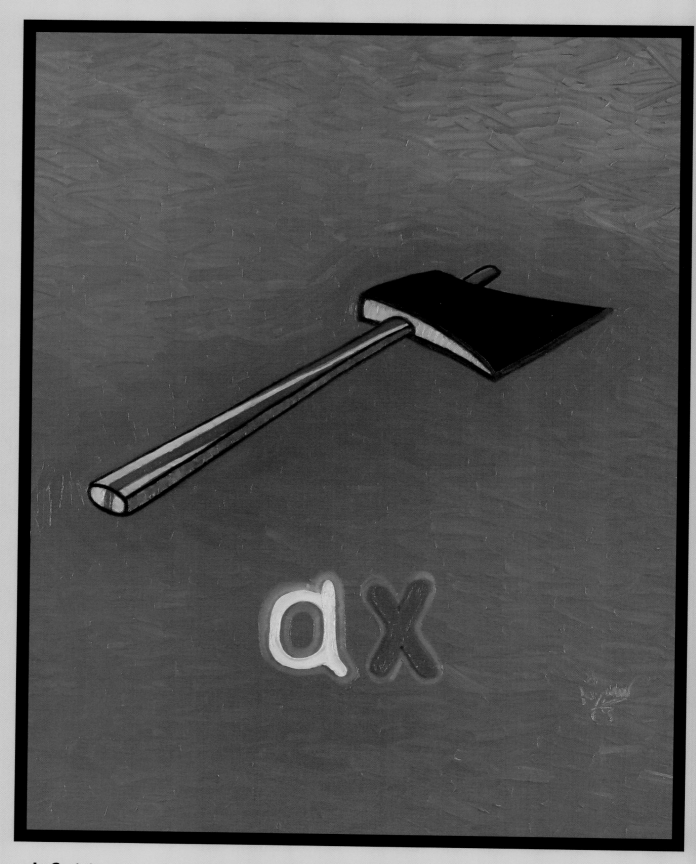

definition > a tool with a metal blade on a long handle, used for cutting wood, felling trees, or chopping objects

idiom > She said she didn't care, but I knew she had an ax to grind.
(an element of revenge, an ulterior aim)

a

A strong and solid tool
is a carefully crafted ax.
It has a grainy, oak handle;
these are just some of the facts.

My father liked to swing his ax
to fell unwanted trees.
In the ice he chopped out holes
to catch fat fish with ease.

Its blade is made of sturdy steel,
tapered to a shocking edge.
It's bold and cold, and painted black;
what a powerful, useful wedge!

axis
mixture
oxygen

hexagon
Mexico
experience

complex
helix
index

69

definition > a small toy that is made of two circular parts joined together that goes up and down a string as you flick your wrist up and down

idiom > Sam behaved like a yo-yo! (to act foolishly)

yo-yo

The yo-yo is a crazy toy,
a spool wound round with string.
You spin it down and reel it back;
wrist flick follows fling!

I play with mine – a brilliant red –
second to minute to hour.
The only time I put it down
is when I take a shower.

Tamika thinks it's a waste of time;
I wonder why she said it?
Could it be she's fooling me
and really just wants to get it?

y

you
your
you're

beyond
canyon
lawyer

vinyard
backyard
courtyard

definition > a man who practices magic

metaphor > Lebron was a wizard on the basketball court.

wizard

The wacky wizard of color
found pleasure in making life bold.
He revealed the magic of rainbows
and other delights untold.

At times he changed red apples to blue,
bringing giggles of silly delight.
Then he would zap the white snow pink,
making it seem not quite right.

Just when you thought you got it straight,
the wizard would throw you a curve.
Life is a fabulous journey,
the thing to do is keep your nerve.

Z

zebra
zenith
zinc

puzzle
citizen
magazine

megahertz
spritz
jazz

consonant blends

bl	br	cl	cr
dr	fl	fr	gl
gr	pl	pr	sc
scr	sk	sl	sm
sn	sp	spr	st
str	sw	tr	tw

2.

consonant blends
two letters, two sounds

definition > a small non-rigid airship, especially used for observation

simile > The blimp glided slowly through the sky like a whale through the sea.

blimp

A blissful and buoyant sight
on a bright and beautiful day,
one blimp with rainbow-like colors
drifted lazily past our café.

Entranced by its silent motion,
seeing it sail through the sky,
we sat and watched and wondered,
"Where is it headed? And why?"

His name was Ferdinand von Zeppelin,
he invented this gas-filled balloon.
He certainly would have been proud
of the flight on that grand afternoon.

bl

blister
blossom
blessing

ablaze
emblem
stumbling

stable
thimble
indelible

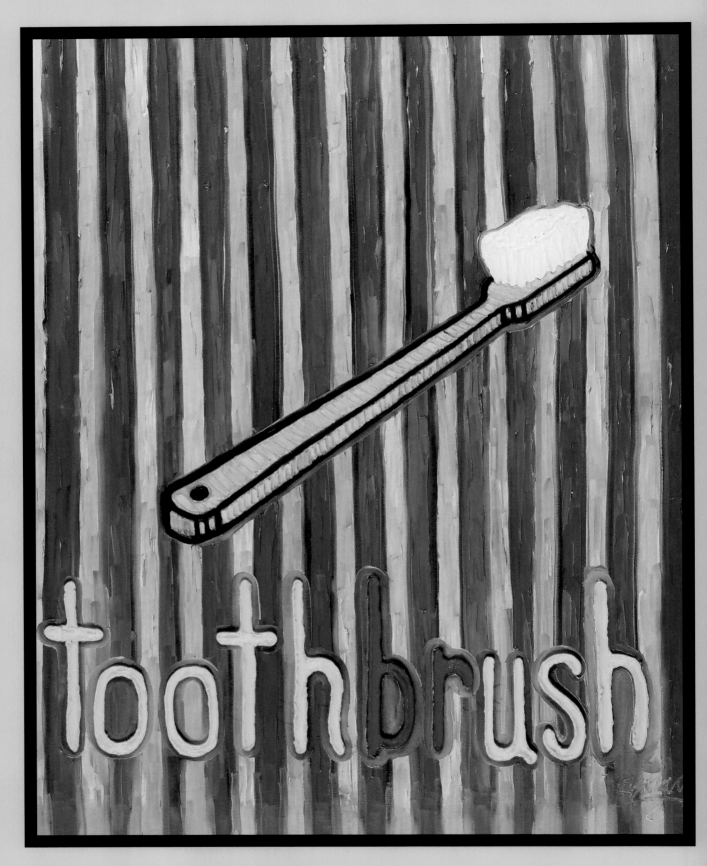

definition > a small brush with bristles made for cleaning your teeth

personification > The toothbrush greeted Max first thing, each and every day.

tooth**br**ush

At attention in its holder,

the toothbrush stands with a yellow grip.

I pick it up and prep it,

squeeze on toothpaste in a strip.

I chose the tickly bristles,

not hard or soft, but medium.

Although I brush them thrice each day,

my teeth don't mind the tedium.

I know it's good to clean my teeth.

I'm asking, "How about you"?

"Of course I brush my teeth," you say,

"and I'm so glad you do too!"

br

breakfast
broccoli
brilliant

a**br**oad
co**br**a
em**br**ace

mem**br**ane
li**br**ary
vi**br**ation

definition > a small piece of curved wire or plastic used for holding pieces of paper together

personification > The paper clip struggled to hold the thick report together.

paper clip

Trying to sort out his papers,

the inventor groaned and grumbled.

They were on the floor and blocked the door,

even more in the corner crumpled.

So he put his mind to thinking

and invented the paper clip.

It was designed of metal to finally settle

his papers in a manageable grip.

Today we use them as intended,

though now many are made of plastic.

All colors, all sizes – they're great organizers –

contraptions so very fantastic!

cl

climax

class

clever

eclipse

conclude

nuclear

exclusion

cycle

tricycle

definition > a type of hard dry bread that is thin and flat

simile > He was so hungry the crackers seemed like a feast fit for a king.

crackers

Salted just right and ready to eat,
crackers are made of unsweetened dough.
They're baked in a very hot oven
to a crispy golden glow.

Delicious with all sorts of soups,
with chunks of good cheese, even better,
and if you're feeling especially nutty,
we can call the peanut butter-getter!

I always bring crackers with me
when I'm going to the zoo.
I can eat them if I'm hungry
and feed Polly the parrot too.

cr

crocodile
crustacean
crayon

re**cr**uit
se**cr**et
de**cr**ee

sa**cr**ed
air**cr**aft
mi**cr**oscope

definition > a tool or machine used for making holes in something hard

simile > Dan worked with the drill like a small child with a new toy.

power drill

Power drills make it easy
to bore out tidy round holes.
They can work on the very hardest of woods,
and can cut into stout, steel poles.

I'm always glad to work with a drill
for projects around the house;
even the quick and simple ones
like hanging a hook for a blouse.

Today I'm headed to buy my drill;
I'm on a meaningful mission.
For me and my sisters owning a drill
will extend the family tradition.

dr

dragon
drama
dream

adrift
hydrate
address

eardrum
dewdrop
hydrogen

85

definition > the colored part of a plant or tree that produces seeds

alliteration > Fresh, fragrant flowers are Florence's favorite.

flowers

The bodacious bouquet of flowers
was a lavender scented surprise.
She appeared delighted and grateful,
emotion shone bright in her eyes.

They went for a walk hand-in-hand
and thought back over the years;
they mingled in all of the memories
and each shed a few caring tears.

To give for the sake of giving
is a moving, empowering thing.
Gestures of kindness enrich us
with the happiness they can bring.

fly
flat
flame

reflect
conflict
influence

rifle
waffle
ruffle

definition > a structure, usually made of wood or metal, that holds or surrounds something such as a picture, door, or window

hyperbole > The antique frame was at least a gazillion years old.

frame

It is an exquisite wooden frame,
an antique seven centuries old,
a vaunted and valued investment,
literally quite good as gold!

The auctioneer started the bidding
at a meek and measly amount.
It would certainly be heading higher,
maybe higher than I can count.

Then it was over and as we expected,
it was Uncle Shel's in the end.
He flagged it, they tagged it,
then home he dragged it.

It's a prize on the wall of his den.

fr

freeze
frozen
fraction

Friday
friendship
frequent

infrequent
afraid
Africa

definition > a lens that produces an enlarged image, typically set in a frame with a handle

idiom > Noah's speakers were put under a magnifying glass by the supervisor.
(to be scrutinized very closely)

magnifying glass

A magnificent glass magnifier
helps us examine and analyze.
We can observe many insects and plants
enlarged for our science-keen eyes.

Our ladybug buddies make very good studies,
contrasting color and more.
Check out their little round bodies.
See details you've not seen before!

So explore this vast world of ours,
unearth and delight in the new,
prepare for the unexpected,
with a unique and wonderful view.

gl

globe
global
glossary

wiggling
hourglass
eyeglasses

angle
single
bugle

definition > a small round green, red, or purple fruit that grows on a vine

alliteration > Grandpa grabbed the green grapes growing on the vine.

grapes

A beautiful bunch of grapes,
fresh off a twisted old vine,
so plump and juicy and sweet,
they're delicious and oh — so divine!

Having or not having seeds,
being purple or red or green,
they're great with breakfast and dinner,
and with everything in between.

These abundant glorious globes
are eaten the whole world over,
from the productive vineyards of Chile
to the chilly Strait of Dover!

gr

gridiron
gravity
gradual

de**gr**ee
en**gr**oss
con**gr**ess

un**gr**ateful
auto**gr**aph
bio**gr**aphy

93

definition > a vehicle that flies by using wings and one or more engines

personification > The airplane climbed above the clouds.

airplane

I took lessons to become a pilot.
I practiced in so many ways.
Now that I've earned my license,
I plan to fly south for days!

Bolivia, Belize and Brazil
are all truly mind-boggling stops.
I'm eager to see the grandeur
of magnificent mountain tops.

I'll know when it's time to return,
my heart will take me back home.
I'll turn the plane to the north,
when I've lost my desire to roam.

pl

plot
place value
please

imply
applause
surplus

complete
perplex
amplify

definition > a desired object given to someone as a gift

alliteration > The pretty present was Hannah's perfect prize.

present

We prepare to open a present
with nervous anticipation;
hoping that when we unwrap it
we'll be feeling great jubilation.

Exchanging gifts is a trendy tradition
for a number of holidays,
for special events around the world,
from Nairobi to faraway bays.

Decked out in decorative paper
with a red and green big bouncy bow,
I'm ready to open this pretty prize.
Try to guess what's inside! Do you know?

pr

predict
prefix
principle

April
impression
expression

appraise
surprise
appropriate

97

scarf

definition > a piece of material worn around the neck or head either for warmth or as an accessory

alliteration > Susan scurried off with the scarlet satin scarf.

scarf

Known by her brilliant red scarf,
she weaves her way about the town,
selling freshly picked flowers
from sunrise to noon to sundown.

A kind and compassionate woman,
she's cherished and loved by all.
Her blossoms bring smiles to townsfolk
from spring to summer to fall.

Sophie's such a special person,
a precious friend whom we adore.
She's been with us almost forever,
so long that she's part of our lore.

SC

scale
sculpture
scavenger

scarlet
fourscore
telescope

underscore
microscope
microscopic

definition > a tool that you use to turn screws

analogy > Screwdriver is to screw as hammer is to nail.

screwdriver

Screwdrivers were invented
for turning and driving a screw.
They're used every day of the week
by a handyman and his crew.

To connect wires to outlets
and make current ready to use,
you needn't think twice, with this turning device,
to hook up electrical juice!

Use it to tighten loose bolts
or install things in their places.
You can even wall a shower stall
or build more storage spaces!

scr

script
scrutinize
scribble

unscrupulous
prescription
inscribe

describe
described
description

101

definition > a pair of long narrow pieces of wood or plastic that you fasten to boots so you can move easily on snow

personification > The skis rested against the wall, patiently awaiting the next run.

skis

I was really ready to rock and roll!
My new skis had been wordlessly waxed.
I was eager with expectations;
I could not begin to relax.

It was a family trip to Lake Tahoe,
a well-known western resort.
I was tutored throughout the morning
and given a "green light" report.

The lift lofted me over old pines;
I pondered the path from the top.
Could I zigzag the Black Diamond?
My goodness! How would I stop?

sk

skill
sky
skeleton

muskrat
whisker
unskilled

mollusk
desk
dusk

103

definition > a light soft shoe that you wear in your house

simile > My slippers are as soft as a down pillow.

slippers

My favorite pair of slippers,
made of striped blue comfortable cloth,
I wear them only indoors;
they slide easily on and off.

Getting up and out of bed,
I slip them on my two cold feet.
With my toes all snugly and warm,
I scurry down for a breakfast treat.

And even in the early spring,
when hardwood floors are much less cold,
Mom says, "Son, wear your slippers!"
Of course, I do as I am told!

sl

slide
slope
slant

sleep
sleeping
slept

enslave
onslaught
landslide

definition > a tall chimney at a factory or on a ship

simile > The smokestack was as tall as a skyscraper.

smokestack

We went on a morning adventure
and cut a new path through the woods.
We gazed with curious eyes,
where the energy complex stood.

A single massive smokestack
was an awesome spewing machine.
It sent billows of smoke – a contrast –
into a sky of baby-blue green.

This tower of power is useful,
keeping homes lighted, warm, and dry.
I'll come back tonight for a splendid sight,
chimney silhouette high in the sky.

smart
smarter
smartest

Mr. Smith
unsmooth
locksmith

blacksmith
nonsmoker
silversmith

definition > a vehicle with sled-like runners used to travel over snow

analogy > Snowmobile is to snow as boat is to water.

snowmobile **sn**

An exciting experience, for sure,

winter fun on cold forest trails,

my snowmobile's so feisty and fast;

why in fact, it practically sails!

Big Blue is my favorite machine;

its size is perfectly right.

It obeys my every command;

turns are thrillingly, chillingly tight.

Well, my mom said, "Always be careful."

My dad said, "Son, don't go too fast."

I foolishly challenged the mountainous woods;

"Would you like to draw on my cast?"

snout
snoring
snooze

snowy
snowman
snowball

sea snail
unsnap
unsnapped

109

definition > a small creature with eight legs that spins webs to catch insects to eat

alliteration > Some species of spiders spin spectacular webs.

spiders

Arachnids are also called spiders.
There are so many thousands of kinds.
With so many different species,
their study will challenge the mind.

The cephalothorax and abdomen,
these are the main body parts.
Eight eyes, eight legs, and a spinneret
provide it with hunting smarts.

You'll discover new webs spun daily.
Watch sticky silk capture the prey!
The web, sharp fangs and venom
bring insects to eat through the day.

sp

sports
specific
special

respond
inspire
respectful

wisp
crisp
grasp

definition > the teeth of a gear used to engage the links of a chain or sprockets of another gear

alliteration > Mr. Springer sells silver sprocket gears.

sprocket

Would you like to look at your bike?
Figure out what makes it move?
You'll find it has many sprockets,
teeth with so many grooves.

Each tooth and groove is a sprocket
that works with the links of a chain.
The rotation is smooth and so steady,
nearly hummms its own sweet refrain.

It's found in the smallest of watches,
and in powerful engines world-wide.
Gears with sprockets can really rock it;
they can make almost anything glide!

spr

sprout
spruce
spread

sprinkle
sprinkled
sprinkling

offspring
wellspring
hairspray

definition > a male chicken

hyperbole > The rooster crowed so loudly the walls of the barn shook.

rooster

The rooster in the barnyard
is green, blue, yellow and red.
His morning "cock-a-doodle-doo!"
gives rise to Sue, Joe and Ted.

The family is suddenly wakened
at the very first light of dawn.
If anyone was still dreaming,
with one crow those dreams are gone.

He's a raucous, walking alarm clock,
punctual and sure at his job.
Strutting his Self all over the yard,
the king of the weave and the bob.

st

state
story
staple

westward
restore
instant

fast
overcast
waist

definition > a soft, sweet, red berry with small, pale seeds on its surface

simile > Simendea was so embarrassed, her face was as red as a strawberry.

116

strawberry

Close your eyes and open your mouth.
Breathe in a very big whiff.
There's a stray strawberry under your nose.
Go ahead! Just take a sniff.

It's red and plump and full of juice,
and packed with Vitamin C.
Taste it! I'm sure once you do,
there'll be a strawberry-eating spree.

Plain or made with shortcake,
enjoy them as you will.
Gleefully gobble them up,
until you've had your fill.

str

straight
strategy
structure

abstract
restrict
awestruck

instrument
astronomy
destruction

sweater

definition > a piece of clothing, often made of wool or cotton, which covers the top half of a person's body

personification > As it hung out to dry, the sweater danced in the wind.

sweater

Wendy wore a woolen sweater
for windy, warm fall walks.
She strolled for hours among beds of flowers,
squinting at wind-borne hawks.

As the winter weather worsened,
and parkas became the norm,
her cardigan was no longer sufficient.
It wouldn't stand up in a storm.

All through that cold and snowy time,
when she donned her sweater indoors,
in her mind's eye she saw happy hawks fly
and conjured colored flowers galore!

SW

switch
sweet
Sweden

swift
swifter
swiftest

windswept
unswayed
unsweetened

definition > a large road vehicle that is used for carrying heavy loads

alliteration > The truck traversed triumphantly through the traffic.

120

truck

We wanted to start a business
aimed at green transportation.
Yes, we thought, an electric truck
can help build a gas-free nation.

Our flagship, stick-shift FLIPSWITCH took off;
our sales were utterly over-the-top.
Demand for this little boxed beauty so strong,
we had to open up shop after shop!

We gained fame around the world
for the revolution we brought about.
The era of battery-powered trucks
was now secured – without a doubt!

tr

triangle
triple
true

cen**tr**al
por**tr**ait
coun**tr**y

en**tr**eaty
con**tr**action
con**tr**adiction

definition > two offspring who are born at the same time to the same mother

analogy > Twins are to two as triplets are to three.

twins

Mighty Max and Silly Sam
are very famous twins;
from all the corners of the earth
they're known for sneaky grins.

Beyond the wooden, brown board fence
they greet us in the morning.
When we play with Max and Sam,
never, ever are they boring.

They sprint and twirl and jump so high
it takes a while to land.
With lots of heart and healthy smiles,
suddenly life is grand.

tw

twitter
twilight
twinkle

twelve
twelfth
twentieth

between
entwine
intertwine

consonant digraphs

ch   ck

gh   kn

ng   ph

sh   th

wh   wr

3.

consonant digraphs
two letters, one sound

definition > a series of connected metal links or rings

idiom > Hans worked so hard it seemed he was chained to his desk. (couldn't get away)

chain

Its owners had to find a way
to make the chemical factory secure;
the broken barrier, which should've been scarier,
had a welcoming, but dangerous allure.

With lots of mighty metal chain
they reinforced that time-worn fence;
bold and heavy three-inch links
were the factory's best defense.

Their message to the neighborhood,
"We'll keep the entrance locked
because we care about the safety
of the children on the block."

ch

change
choice
cheek

exchange
merchant
purchase

inch
branch
stretch

definition > a mechanism that keeps a door, drawer, or gate fastened or shut and is typically opened with a key

idiom > Tonya sold everything – lock, stock and barrel – and sailed around the world. (taking or including everything)

lock

When Sam and I were little kids,
dad bought a lock of steel;
he bolted up the shack out back
where all the paint had peeled.

Years and years and years went by;
his secret was safe in the shed.
Though we'd discovered a path out back,
we knew not where it led.

Right after we turned seventeen,
we both learned how to drive.
With a mighty thwack dad opened the shack;
our ride had been hidden inside!

A jeep! For us! High five!

bucket
jacket
socket

beckon
package
necklace

check
o'clock
hammock

definition > a long narrow boxlike container used to hold water or food for animals

metaphor > The horses' trough was an oasis on the dusty, desert farm.

130

trough

A classic, weathered wooden trough,
constructed years ago,
is where the horses go to drink
in sunshine and in snow.

Grandpa built it sure and strong
with timber he cut down;
it was made of solid maple planks
and painted deep, dark brown.

Nellie and Sadie trot right up;
they need not be coerced.
Their heads thrown back, then down to drink,
they satisfy their thirst.

gh

cough
coughed
coughing

laugh
laughter
laughing

tough
tougher
toughest

definition > a bag that you wear on your shoulders, which is used to carry objects

hyperbole > Ethan's knapsack was so heavy it must have had a ton of books inside it.

knapsack

It's time to leave for school
and Sam is ready to go.
He waves goodbye to mom
and leaves with a flair and a flow.

A stylish bag on his shoulders,
he travels forth with ease.
This early autumn morning
he feels content and pleased.

In his bright, red knapsack
are laptop, pencils and paper,
plus a king-sized chocolate bar,
a very clever caper.

kn

know
knew
knowledge

knee
kneel
knight

knickknack
unknown
doorknob

133

definition > a piece of jewelry that you wear on your finger

analogy > Ring is to finger as bracelet is to wrist.

ring

At Marta's quinceanera,
grandma held a box in her hand.
An heirloom ring to be a surprise
was what Abuela had planned.

The ring was set with an oyster's pearl,
a smooth and shiny white.
It had blue prongs all around it.
Its luster was pure and bright.

Whenever Marta wore the ring,
a treasure from ocean water,
she honored grandma's loving gift,
that one day she'd give her daughter.

ng

long
longer
longest

sing
singer
singing

cling
clang
clung

definition > an instrument for the transmission of sound or speech to a distant point

analogy > Telephone is to voice as telegraph is to code.

tele**ph**one

Alexander Graham Bell and his friend,
Tom Watson was his name,
aimed to send voice over wire;
"Success!" they would soon proclaim.

In eighteen seventy-six,
the words they transmitted were few;
said Alexander to Thomas,
"Mr. Watson, come here. I want you!"

Their work moved along very quickly,
a dial, a ring, a tone.
Can you guess what it is they invented?
Yup, you're right! It's the telephone.

ph

phoenix
physical
phonics

s**ph**ere
hy**ph**en
epi**ph**any

trium**ph**
paragra**ph**
autogra**ph**

definition > an aircraft designed to travel between Earth and outer space

hyperbole > The space shuttle's take-off was so loud it could be heard half way around the world.

space
shuttle

Our minds were completely made up.
We would stand together, undaunted.
We longed for a launch at Cape Kennedy;
it was truly all that we wanted.

So we begged and pleaded, pined and whined;
we simply refused to back off.
"Oh, please pretty please, mom and dad,
can we see the space shuttle blast-off?"

Wow! Our parents took us out to the site.
The shuttle exploded away from its base.
With a roar it soared to places unexplored,
taking astronauts to their station in space.

sh

shuttled
shadow
shampoo

sunshine
sweatshirt
friendship

Spanish
abolish
angelfish

definition > a sharp point that grows on the stem of a plant such as a rose

idiom > Michael was a thorn in my side. (an annoying, disturbing, troubling thing)

thorn

Though radiant roses have thorns,
terribly sharp wooden spines,
they often adorn our gardens,
creating myriad magical lines.

There's something very romantic
about a single red, red rose;
but it satisfies, it gratifies,
seeing the garden where it grows.

I went out back at my uncle's
and strolled through a trellis of vines.
Explosions of rose met my eyes and nose;
sight and scent were both sweet and sublime!

there
their
they're

anthology
anything
weather

eighth
ninth
tenth

definition > a small cart with one wheel in the front and two long handles, used to carry things outdoors

personification > Grandpa Jonah's old wheelbarrow groaned each time it carried a load.

wheelbarrow

If you've got a task that makes you ask,
"How do I move this across the yard?"
Some people you've met will tell you to get
a wheelbarrow, "Then it won't be too hard."

You can wheel it here and wheel it there,
filled with bulbs and plants and flowers.
It's very strong, you can move it along,
in sunshine or in spring showers.

A wheelbarrow, a wagon, a handcart,
it's the workhorse of any backyard.
Everything's hauled, the work's done for all,
leaving the wheelbarrow standing guard.

wh

wheat
whale
whisper

cart**wh**eel
mean**wh**ile
over**wh**elm

no**wh**ere
some**wh**ere
any**wh**ere

143

definition > an instrument worn on the wrist that is used to tell time

personification > The wrist watch whispered time with each tick of the hand –
second by second, minute after minute.

wristwatch

Oh no, I'm late to school again!
Teacher acts like it's a crime.
So if you please, for my birthday,
I'd like a wristwatch to measure time.

Why, when I have a watch
I'll never again be late;
I'll know if it's seven-thirty
or – oops – already quarter to eight!

I'd like a watch with a bright blue rim,
with a band of bright orange plaid.
I'd arrive at school right on the hour,
thinking, "Jenny, you are totally rad!"

And Mr. Smith wouldn't be mad!

wr

write
wrote
written

wreath
wrinkle
wreckage

a**wr**y
play**wr**ight
type**wr**itten

vowel digraphs

au	aw
oi	oy
oo	oo
ou	ow

4.

vowel digraphs
two letters, one sound

definition > a four-wheeled motor vehicle used for road travel

simile > Eve's automobile was built like a tank.

automobile **au**

It's the first automobile I've purchased,
waxed and glistening and new.
I ordered my favorite color,
miraculous midnight blue.

They called to say it was ready
on a cold and blustery day.
My plan was to drive to the mountains
where we'd ski and skate and sleigh.

The moment soon arrived,
my family was ready to go.
With all of our bags packed in the trunk,
we were jazzed to go to the snow.

author
audience
auditorium

faucet
caucus
sausage

exhaust
applaud
overhaul

definition > a thin tube made of plastic or paper used for sucking a drink from a bottle or glass

simile > The straw was as pink as a peony.

straw

Samar's favorite slender straw
for slurping a long cold drink,
is a simple one made of plastic,
a riotously reddish pink.

At times she sips so slowly;
at times she enjoys a good gulp.
Though she may not care, she'll sure be aware
if the straw gets clogged with pulp!

When summer comes she loves to drink
frosty soda or cold lemonade.
She swigs with her straw,
says with a slight guffaw,
"I've got it made in the shade."

aw

awe
awkward
awning

hawk
squawk
dawning

law
draw
thaw

definition > round pieces of money made of metal

idiom > It is important that Andrew and Aaron see both sides of the coin. (paying attention to opposing viewpoints)

coins

Max and Sam had an uncle
who was charming and charismatic.
His favorite thing was collecting coins,
a hobby fanatically fantastic!

He proudly showed them two old coins,
quite odd and extremely rare;
he had purchased them many years before
at the Rhinebeck County Fair.

Uncle Charles told Sam and Max,
"These are centuries-old doubloons!"
They giggled and wriggled,
while on paper they squiggled
pictures of pirates with swords and harpoons.

oi

ointment
oily
oilcloth

v**oi**ce
j**oi**st
sp**oi**l

turm**oi**l
disapp**oi**nt
aster**oi**d

definition > objects used by children to play

alliteration > Troy's toys were totally terrific.

toys

My Legos, Jin's truck, Chin's rabbit,
those are our very favorite toys.
It's raining, we're playing inside,
making boisterous loud boy noise.

Chin's bunny hops about my room.
Jin's truck goes round in laps.
I build towers with my Legos.
Then Mom says, "Time for naps!"

"Aw Mom, but we're still playing;
my tower has only six floors."
"Well, son Hop, after nap the rain will stop!
And you can take your toys outdoors."

oy

oyster
oysters
joyful

loyal
royalty
annoying

destroy
employ
corduroy

155

definition > an object shaped like a small wheel wound with wire or thread

hyperbole > Anthoula's spool was wound with miles of thread.

sp**oo**l

Mother has a flowered box
where she keeps her stuff for sewing;
inside it there are buttons and threads,
in piles overflowing.

The threads are of every color,
wound tightly around a spool.
I can look and play and build with them;
but no unwinding! That's her rule.

Yesterday, while playing outside
I somehow tore my shirt;
"No worries, Raj, I'll sew it up
while you go eat dessert!

oo

ooze
school
mood

noon
afternoon
booboo

zoo
cuckoo
bamboo

157

definition > a curved object, usually metal or plastic, on which things are hung

hyperbole > The hook in Tony's closet is so strong an elephant could hang from it by its trunk!

158

hook

A curved and functional hook,
crafted of very strong metal,
can be used to hang many things,
from a coat to a hat to a kettle.

My coat is a slippery slicker,
and to keep it up off the floor,
there's a hook conveniently placed
right next to our main entrance door.

There's a hook for the hat in my closet,
for the kettle that hangs over the sink,
without this clever invention,
imagine the thoughts we'd have to think.

oo

book
hoof
brook

cookie
rookie
wooden

afoot
driftwood
understood

159

definition > a building that you live in, especially one that is intended to be used by a family

hyperbole > Ashley and Amanda were blinded by the sun reflecting off the brightly colored houses!

houses

A row of colorful houses
sprout up in a field of green;
with the sun brightly shining above them,
it's a scene from a peaceful dream.

The architects, if you can believe this,
are none other than Sam and Max!
Their new design, which is hard to define,
makes it tough to tell fronts from backs!

People who are driving by them
love to watch as the evening sun fades;
a sight to behold – colors all turn to gold –
mixed with beautiful rainbow shades.

ou

ounce
outdoors
outlook

noun
ground
mountain

pronoun
council
boundary

clown

definition > a performer who wears make-up and funny clothes and tries to make people laugh, especially in a circus

idiom > Quit clowning around! (acting in a way that is not serious)

clown

Bobo the orange-haired clown,
a comic communicator,
enjoys a certain renown,
from cold Poles to the hot equator.

Wearing a colorful costume,
with make-up all over his face,
he carries his bag of tricks
in his oversized overnight case.

Clever and zany and silly,
outlandish, with a big red nose,
this jokester turns everything upside down.
His world is totally transposed!

OW

crowd

brown

vowel

shower

chowder

downward

vow

endow

snowplow

r-controlled vowels

ar

er

ir

or

ur

5.

r-controlled vowels
two letters, one sound

definition > a round glass container with a lid, used for storing things

analogy > Jar is to jam as bottle is to water.

166

jar

We sauntered into the sand,
picking beach plums to make preserves;
and later readied the jars we'd use
to build our jam reserves.

We cooked the fruit with sugar and water,
added lemon and pectin, all mixed.
Then we sterilized the Ball jars and lids
for jam from the beach plums we picked.

With plums, and black and blue berries,
gathered on the craggy Maine coast,
we made jamming jars of jelly.
I think I'll have mine with toast!

ar

artichoke
artist
arctic

garden
harmony
Antarctica

par
star
guitar

definition > a plant with green leaves shaped like large feathers

metaphor > The ferns were a sea of green covering the forest floor.

fern

A green and flowerless flora
is abundant throughout the Northwest,
searching there for a rare one
makes for a wonderful quest.

Ferns are remarkable plants,
sprinkling tiny round spores.
We find them all over the globe,
nestled deep on the verdant tree floors.

Shielded from the searing sun
by the canopy overhead,
thriving on nature's nutrients,
is a delicate foliage well-fed.

er

verb
adverb
average

Mercury
perspective
intersecting

perimeter
character
liter

definition > a female child

simile > Jade's smile was as bright as a star.

girl

Banjit had an assignment
to study a far east nation.
And so she began an exploration of facts
surrounding the Thai population.

It was her grandparents who came
across from Siam way back in 'thirty-four.
Their stories and values had inspired the girl;
now was her time to learn more.

She read many books and tales online;
her report was well-researched and written.
It was laced with interviews from Ya and Pu.
Ah, Thailand! She was simply smitten!

irk
irregular
irruption

circuit
affirm
thirsty

sir
fir
whir

definition > a tall plant with yellow seeds, harvested in the fall

alliteration > Carlos concocted a creamy corn casserole.

corn

A just-picked ear of corn
smells clean and fresh and yummy,
smothered in butter and salt,
what a treat for a hungry tummy!

We went to the fields this morning;
the dayspring air was so sweet.
We checked for the longest silk tassels,
the ears that would be most complete.

Won't you please join us this evening,
to share in our summer delight.
I can tell from the smile on your face,
that we'll see you for dinner tonight.

or

organic
orchestra
organization

north
forward
perform

doctor
alligator
conductor

definition > a bag used to carry money and personal items

personification > The purse hugged Lena's shoulder like an old friend.

purse

A purse can be called a handbag,
a pocketbook or two-handle tote.
It's used to store special things,
even a well-worn, torn love note.

Purses are all shapes and sizes;
some are stylish and very high fashion.
Made of cloth or fine leather,
for some a purse is a passion!

It closes with zippers or Velcro,
with buttons, snaps or a string;
whatever the close is, the one that you chose is
the one that holds every last thing!

ur

urgent
urban
urchin

purpose
surface
Thursday

murmur
concur
sulfur

cv̆c

cv̄

cv̄ce̸

cv̄/vc

ˆvr

cle̸

6.

rules, lists, strategies

six basic syllable spelling patterns

syllable spelling patterns word lists

onset-rime word lists

prefixes, suffixes, roots word lists

learning strategies

six basic syllable spelling patterns

CV̆C (Closed Syllable)

This syllable spelling pattern ends in a consonant.

The vowel sound is generally short.

This is called a **closed syllable.**

sand	leg	win	pot	just
what	won	put (rule breakers)		
dan/cer	ten/der	dis/cuss	mon/ster	sun/shine
lad/der	pen/ny	hid/den	bot/tom	sup/per
bin/der	grin/der	man/ger (rule breakers)		

CV̄ (Open Syllable)

This syllable spelling pattern ends in a vowel.

The vowel sound is generally long.

This is called an **open syllable**.

cra/zy	de/pend	fi/nal	mo/bile	cu/test
wa/ter	ma/chine	bu/sy (rule breakers)		

CV̄C̶e̶ (Vowel-Consonant-Silent e Syllable)

This syllable spelling pattern ends with a silent e.

The vowel sound is generally long.

This is called a **vowel-consonant -silent e syllable.**

game	Pete	dime	bone	fuse
in/vade	de/lete	side/way	hope/less	a/muse
have	some	done (rule breakers)		

C̄V̸C (Vowel Team Syllable)

This syllable spelling pattern has a vowel digraph (two letters, one sound). The first vowel sound is generally long and the second vowel is silent. Such vowel teams include ai, ay, ea, ee, ew, ie, oa, ow, and ui. This is called a **vowel team syllable**.

rain	seed	bean	goat	fruit
Mon/day	snow/ball	mag/pie	car/load	sun/beam
said	been	great	(rule breakers)	

V̂r (R-Controlled Vowel Syllable)

This syllable spelling pattern has a vowel followed by an r, and the r affects the sound of the vowel.
The vowel and the r appear in the same syllable.
This is called an **r-controlled vowel syllable**.

art/ist	per/fect	thirst/y	or/gan	pur/pose

cl̸é (Consonant + le Syllable)

This syllable spelling pattern appears at the end of a word.
It is the only syllable without a vowel sound.
This is called a **consonant + le syllable**.

sam/ple	trem/ble	thim/ble	bot/tle	mus/cle
ta/ble	ri/fle	ti/tle	bri/dle	bu/gle

syllable pattern word lists

c̆v̆c pattern	c̄v̄ pattern	c̄v̄c¢ pattern
1. pat/tern	fla/vor	base/ball
2. Sat/urn	na/tion	fe/male
3. sen/tence	be/tween	com/pete
4. Jen/ney	re/main	com/plete
5. pic/ture	sci/ence	nine/ty
6. bit/ter	qui/et	de/cide
7. job/less	mo/tion	smoke/stack
8. hot/ter	fro/zen	note/book
9. sub/ject	pu/pil	use/ful
10. sum/mer	mu/sic	re/fuse

c̄v̸c pattern	v̂r pattern	cl̸é pattern
1. pain/ful	par/ka	fa/ble
2. thumb/nail	star/light	ma/ple
3. sea/weed	per/fect	gen/tle
4. oat/meal	ger/bil	ped/dle
5. die/hard	cir/cus	nic/kle
6. un/tie	thir/teen	mid/dle
7. road/side	bor/der	no/ble
8. ap/proach	for/ty	wob/ble
9. fruit/ful	tur/key	puz/zle
10. un/glue	pur/chase	tur/tle

onset-rime word lists
the vowel letter a

ace	face	race	place
ack	back	sack	crack
ade	fade	made	blade
ail	mail	pail	tail
ain	pain	rain	brain
air	hair	pair	stair
ake	lake	cake	take
ale	sale	tale	whale
ame	came	game	name
ank	bank	sank	drank
ap	cap	tap	flap
ark	bark	dark	park
ash	smash	crash	cash
ate	plate	gate	late
aw	paw	claw	jaw
ay	day	way	play

onset-rime word lists
the vowel letter e

each	beach	teach	peach
eak	speak	leak	weak
eal	meal	deal	steal
eam	dream	beam	team
ear	hear	dear	year
eat	beat	seat	neat
eed	bleed	feed	seed
een	teen	green	queen
ell	bell	tell	fell
en	Ken	den	hen
end	send	bend	lend
ent	bent	sent	went
ept	kept	slept	crept
est	best	rest	nest
ew	new	flew	chew
ex	hex	Rex	flex

onset-rime word lists
the vowel letter i

ice	price	nice	mice
ick	kick	thick	sick
id	hid	Sid	bid
ide	hide	side	slide
ig	big	twig	wig
ight	might	light	tight
ill	pill	grill	fill
im	Tim	slim	rim
ime	dime	slime	mime
in	pin	grin	win
ine	nine	pine	dine
ink	drink	pink	sink
int	print	mint	hint
ip	dip	grip	slip
ist	twist	mist	list
it	split	sit	knit

184

onset-rime word lists

the vowel letter o

oat	boat	coat	moat
ock	clock	rock	shock
oist	moist	joist	hoist
oke	joke	broke	spoke
on	ton	won	son
one	tone	phone	stone
op	pop	top	shop
ope	scope	rope	hope
oop	hoop	scoop	troop
ore	store	more	sore
ot	shot	got	not
ote	note	tote	vote
ound	sound	found	round
ow	know	tow	show
ow	how	cow	pow
own	crown	brown	town

onset-rime word lists

the vowel letter u

ub	rub	tub	shrub
uck	truck	duck	luck
ue	clue	due	glue
uddle	puddle	muddle	fuddle
udge	fudge	smudge	budge
ug	mug	rug	tug
ule	mule	rule	yule
ull	pull	full	bull
um	plum	gum	sum
ump	pump	bump	jump
un	sun	fun	bun
unch	crunch	lunch	punch
unk	trunk	shrunk	junk
ush	rush	brush	hush
ust	must	trust	gust
ut	shut	cut	nut

prefixes, suffixes, and roots lists

parts with meaning

prefix	meaning	usage
anti	against	antiwar
bi	two	bicycle
extra	more, beyond	extraordinary
pre	before	preschool
re	again	review
tele	distant	telephone
un	not	unbelievable

suffix	meaning	usage
able, ible	capable of	portable, legible
ation	that which is	irritation
cy	state of being	democracy
fy	to enlarge	magnify
ize	to make	harmonize
or	person who	advisor
ous	full of	mountainous

root	meaning	usage
aud	sound	audiotape
dic	peak, say	dictate
geo	earth	geography
graph	writing, print	biography
hydro, hydr	water	hydroelectric
spec	look	spectator
therm	heat	thermometer

making words strategy
finding spelling patterns

first

Pick a multi-syllable word from the word list next to the poem or a multi-syllable word from within the poem. Rearrange the letters of the word at the top of a paper in alphabetical order.

Wednesday

a, d, d, e, e, n, s, w, y

next

See how many words you can make with these letters. Start with a two or three letter word. Then make more words by adding, subtracting, or substituting a letter or letter combination. You can only use the letters from the original word. In this case, *Wednesday*. When there are no more words to be made from the two or three letter word you started with, then begin again with another two or three letter word, or a larger word.

an, Dan, den, end, ends, send,
weed, seed, need, needs, needy, deed, dead, dew,
new, yew, sew, sewn, yes, Wes, see, we, day, way, say,
sway, nay, dye, eye, dense, sandy, dandy, Sweden

then

Take your words that have common spelling patterns and sort them into categories. After that, sort the words that are related.

- ay	- eed	- ew
day	weed	dew
way	seed	new
say	need	yew
need	needs	needy

finally

To finish the word play, "transfer" your understanding and come up with words that are related to the words created. You can now use any letters of the alphabet.

needlessly   Swedish   density

word ladder strategy
finding spelling patterns

pick one word and play

Choose a word made from the "making words strategy.
Start with just one simple three or four letter word and see how
many words you can create by adding, subtracting, or substituting
a letter or letter combination.   Use any letter of the alphabet.

Dan
den
end
send
bend
band
land
sand
say
slay
clay
day
dam
yam
jam
jar
tar
star
start
starter

syllabication word study strategy

syllabicating a word

syllables

Without a strategy for chunking longer words into smaller parts, students may look at a multi-syllable word and simply resort to guessing what it is — or altogether skipping it. Syllables are the building blocks of words. Syllables have a vowel sound, and only one vowel sound (except for the *consonant + le syllable*, which has no vowel sound). Knowing the basic six syllable patterns and hearing the vowel sound within a syllable helps readers to sound out and spell words. Being able to automatically sound out longer words enables us to develop reading fluency. And it is reading fluency that frees-up the reader's brainpower to read for comprehension and make meaning.

purpose

Work with words from the poems and word lists to apply the basic six syllable spelling patterns and the 18 vowel sounds of the English language to sound out and spell words.

one

Dot vowels that make a sound, but not vowels that are silent.

two

Sound out the syllables and divide them with a slash.

three

Mark each syllable with one of the six basic syllable spelling patterns, or show the actual spelling of the sounds if it is a rule breaker (e.i., -sion).

four

Box a suffix if there is one.

five

Add other notes that show your ability to take a word and break it apart.

Remember, just as there are "rule breaker" words (said), there are "rule breaker" syllables (-sion).

poem
word study
strategy
measuring the beat of a poem

purpose

Play with the poems to understand that poetry has a meter, which is a pattern based on the number of syllables per line. This helps to develop phonemic awareness of the syllables within words.

tw

Mighty Max and Silly Sam
are very famous twins.
From all the corners of the earth
they're known for sneaky grins.

Beyond the wooden, brown board fence
they greet us in the morning.
When we play with Max and Sam,
never, ever are they boring.

They sprint and twirl and jump so high
it takes a while to land.
With lots of heart and healthy smiles,
suddenly life is grand.

Line	# of Syllables
1	7
2	6
3	8
4	6
5	8
6	7
7	7
8	8
9	8
10	6
11	8
12	6

one

Read each line aloud and count the number of syllables.

two

List the number of syllables per line.

three

Think about and discuss the syllable pattern of each stanza.

fluency
strategy
exercising fluency, expression, pace

purpose

To read with fluency means reading smoothly and accurately, without pausing to figure out words. We identify words automatically. When we read with fluency, we can focus on the meaning of the text, rather than word recognition. Fluent readers comprehend better than non-fluent readers. It is important that readers practice and develop their reading fluency. Reading the same passage several times improves fluency.

one

Read the poem silently (repeated readings).
Aim to read with fluency, expression, and pace.

two

Read the poem aloud (repeated readings).
Aim to read with volume, clarity, fluency, expression, and pace.

three

Present the poem to an audience or on video (repeated presentations).
Aim to present with the Traits of Presentation:
> volume and clarity
> fluency, expression, and pace
> body language and eye contact

definitions

fluency   read smoothly and accurately

expression   read with tones of emotion, attitude, and energy

pace   read slowing down, speeding up, or pausing for effect

volume   read with the appropriate loudness of voice

clarity   read with a clear enunciation of words

eye contact   present with a direct look to engage the audience

body language   present with body and hand movements

vocabulary strategy
understanding the meaning of a word
purpose
Understanding the meaning of words helps readers comprehend precisely and accurately. Learning vocabulary with word web thinking helps us to build and shape our understanding of the meaning of a word.

one
Pick a word.

two
Complete the word web.

three
Engage in conversation to build an understanding of the word.

word web

(word)

(is)	(is not)

(definition in your own words)

(example)	(non-example)

(syllabication)

(dictionary definition)

(part of speech)

(word used in a sentence)

literal comprehension strategy
retelling just the facts

purpose

Learning to retell and summarize what is read, we develop our literal comprehension and build language capacity. Summarizing a story, we focus on retelling the elements of a story - characters, setting, conflict, and resolution, and plot. Summarizing an information text, we focus on retelling the main ideas and supporting details determined to be most important.

one

Read the poem.

two

For a story, think about the characters, setting, conflict, resolution and plot. For an information text, think about the main idea and supporting details determined to be most important.

three

For a story, retell the setting, characters, and events.
For information, retell who or what did what, where, when, why, and how; focus on main ideas and important supporting details.

definitions

character   a person, imaginary being, or animal in a story

setting   the time, place, and surroundings where a story takes place - including the past, present, and future

event   something that occurs in a certain place at a particular moment - a happening that takes place

main idea   an over arching idea, supported with details

supporting detail   facts and pieces of information supportive of the main idea

inferential comprehension strategy

thinking what might be true

purpose

By reading between the lines, and putting two and two together, we aim to think about what is implied - what else might be true. We bring together background knowledge, personal experience, and meaning across the text to make inferences supported by evidence.

one

Read the poem.

two

Think what might be true beyond the words.
Make an inference supported by evidence.

three

Engage in conversation to share your thinking.

definitions

visualize   form a detailed sensory or emotional images in the mind that go beyond the words

make connections   know a relationship between the information presented and yourself, people, the world, or another text (text-to-self, text-to-world, text-to-text)

infer   tell what is implied or suggest a conclusion based upon evidence from the text combined with background knowledge and personal experience

the

of

and

a

to

7.

sight words
10 lists of 100

sight words
first 100

	1.	2.	3.	4.	5.
A.	the	of	and	a	to
B.	in	you	that	he	was
C.	for	on	are	as	with
D.	his	they	I	at	be
E.	this	have	from	or	one
F.	had	by	words	but	not
G.	what	all	were	we	when
H.	your	can	said	there	use
I.	an	each	which	she	do
J.	how	their	if	will	up
K.	other	about	out	many	then
L.	them	these	so	some	her
M.	would	make	like	him	into
N.	time	has	look	two	more
O.	write	go	see	no	way
P.	could	people	my	than	first
Q.	water	been	called	who	oil
R.	sit	now	find	long	day
S.	did	get	come	made	may
T.	part	down	number	is	it

sight words
second 100

	1.	2.	3.	4.	5.
A.	over	new	sound	take	only
B.	little	work	know	place	years
C.	live	me	back	give	most
D.	very	after	thing	our	just
E.	name	good	man	think	say
F.	great	where	help	through	much
G.	before	line	right	too	means
H.	old	any	same	tell	boy
I.	follow	came	want	show	also
J.	around	form	three	small	set
K.	put	end	does	well	large
L.	must	big	even	turn	her
M.	why	ask	went	men	read
N.	need	land	home	us	move
O.	try	kind	hand	picture	again
P.	change	off	play	spell	air
Q.	away	animal	house	point	page
R.	letter	mother	answer	found	study
S.	learn	should	America	sentence	world
T.	another	because	different	late	it's

sight words
third 100

	1.	2.	3.	4.	5.
A.	high	every	near	add	food
B.	between	own	below	country	plant
C.	last	school	father	keep	tree
D.	never	start	city	earth	eyes
E.	light	thought	head	under	story
F.	saw	left	don't	few	while
G.	along	might	close	something	seem
H.	next	hard	open	example	begin
I.	life	always	those	both	paper
J.	together	got	group	often	run
K.	important	until	children	side	feet
L.	car	mile	might	walk	white
M.	sea	began	grow	took	river
N.	four	carry	state	once	book
O.	hear	stop	without	second	late
P.	miss	idea	enough	eat	face
Q.	watch	far	Indian	real	almost
R.	let	above	girl	sometimes	its
S.	mountains	cut	young	talk	soon
T.	list	song	being	leave	family

sight words
fourth 100

	1.	2.	3.	4.	5.
A.	body	music	color	stand	sun
B.	questions	fish	area	mark	dog
C.	horse	birds	problem	complete	room
D.	knew	since	ever	piece	told
E.	usually	didn't	friends	easy	heard
F.	order	red	door	become	sure
G.	top	ship	across	today	during
H.	short	better	best	however	low
I.	hours	black	products	happened	whole
J.	measure	remember	early	reached	waves
K.	listen	wind	rock	covered	space
L.	fast	several	toward	himself	hold
M.	five	morning	passed	vowel	true
N.	hundred	against	pattern	numeral	table
O.	north	slowly	money	map	farm
P.	pulled	draw	voice	seen	cold
Q.	cried	plan	notice	south	sing
R.	war	ground	fall	king	town
S.	I'll	unit	figure	certain	field
T.	travel	wood	fire	upon	step

sight words
fifth 100

	1.	2.	3.	4.	5.
A.	built	done	English	road	half
B.	ten	fly	gave	box	finally
C.	wait	correct	oh	quickly	person
D.	became	shown	minutes	strong	verb
E.	stars	front	feel	fact	inches
F.	street	decided	contain	less	course
G.	surface	produce	building	ocean	class
H.	note	nothing	include	carefully	rest
I.	scientists	inside	wheels	stay	green
J.	known	island	week	machine	base
K.	ago	stood	plane	system	ran
L.	behind	round	boat	game	force
M.	understand	warm	brought	common	bring
N.	explain	dry	though	language	shape
O.	deep	thousands	equation	clear	yes
P.	government	yet	filled	heat	full
Q.	hot	check	object	am	rule
R.	among	noun	power	cannot	able
S.	six	size	dark	material	ball
T.	special	heavy	fine	pair	circle

sight words
sixth 100

	1.	2.	3.	4.	5.
A.	matter	square	syllables	perhaps	can't
B.	direction	felt	suddenly	test	bill
C.	center	farmers	ready	anything	blue
D.	general	energy	subject	Europe	moon
E.	region	return	believe	members	dance
F.	picked	simple	cells	paint	mind
G.	love	cause	rain	exercise	eggs
H.	train	divided	wish	developed	drop
I.	window	difference	distance	heart	sit
J.	sum	summer	probably	forest	wall
K.	legs	sat	main	winter	wide
L.	written	length	reason	interest	kept
M.	arms	brother	beautiful	present	race
N.	store	job	edge	past	sign
O.	discovered	finished	record	wild	happy
P.	beside	gone	sky	grass	million
Q.	instrument	west	weather	root	lay
R.	meet	third	months	paragraph	raised
S.	represent	soft	whether	clothes	shall
T.	flowers	teacher	held	describe	drive

sight words
seventh 100

	1.	2.	3.	4.	5.
A.	cross	speak	solve	appear	metal
B.	son	either	ice	sleep	village
C.	factors	result	jumped	snow	ride
D.	care	floor	hill	pushed	baby
E.	buy	century	outside	everything	tall
F.	already	instead	phrase	soil	bed
G.	copy	free	hope	spring	case
H.	laughed	nation	quite	themselves	type
I.	remain	bright	lead	everyone	lake
J.	method	section	iron	within	hair
K.	dictionary	age	amount	scale	pounds
L.	although	per	broken	moment	tiny
M.	possible	gold	milk	quiet	act
N.	bottom	stone	natural	build	middle
O.	speed	count	constant	someone	sail
P.	rolled	bear	wonder	smiled	angle
Q.	fraction	Africa	killed	melody	lot
R.	trip	hole	poor	let's	fight
S.	surprise	French	exactly	beat	died
T.	temperature	dress	fingers	couldn't	cat

sight words
eighth 100

	1.	2.	3.	4.	5.
A.	row	least	catch	climbed	wrote
B.	shouted	continued	itself	else	plains
C.	gas	England	burning	design	joined
D.	foot	law	ears	grass	you're
E.	grew	skin	valley	cents	key
F.	president	brown	trouble	cool	cloud
G.	lost	sent	symbols	wear	bad
H.	save	experiment	engine	drawing	alone
I.	information	choose	single	touch	east
J.	express	mouth	decimal	equal	yard
K.	decimal	yourself	control	practice	report
L.	straight	rise	statement	stick	party
M.	seeds	suppose	woman	coast	bank
N.	period	wire	pay	clean	visit
O.	bit	whose	received	garden	please
P.	strange	caught	fell	team	God
Q.	captain	direct	serve	child	desert
R.	increase	history	business	cost	maybe
S.	separate	break	uncle	hunting	flow
T.	lady	students	human	feeling	art

sight words
ninth 100

	1.	2.	3.	4.	5.
A.	supply	corner	electric	insects	crops
B.	tone	provide	sand	doctor	hit
C.	thus	won't	cook	bones	tall
D.	board	modern	compound	mine	wasn't
E.	fit	addition	belong	soldiers	safe
F.	guess	silent	trade	rather	fun
G.	compare	crowd	poem	enjoy	flat
H.	elements	indicate	except	expect	seven
I.	interesting	sense	string	blow	famous
J.	value	wings	movement	exciting	pole
K.	branches	thick	blood	lie	spot
L.	bell	loud	consider	suggested	thin
M.	position	entered	fruit	tied	rich
N.	dollars	send	sight	Japanese	chief
O.	stream	planets	rhythm	eight	tube
P.	major	observe	science	necessary	weight
Q.	meat	lifted	process	army	hat
R.	property	particular	swim	terms	park
S.	current	sell	shoulder	industry	wash
T.	block	spread	cattle	wife	sharp

sight words
tenth 100

	1.	2.	3.	4.	5.
A.	company	radio	we'll	action	capital
B.	factories	settled	yellow	isn't	truck
C.	southern	fair	printed	wouldn't	ahead
D.	chance	born	level	triangle	rose
E.	molecules	France	repeated	column	sir
F.	western	church	sister	oxygen	plural
G.	various	agreed	opposite	wrong	chart
H.	prepared	pretty	solution	fresh	shop
I.	suffix	especially	shoes	actually	nose
J.	afraid	dead	sugar	adjective	fig
K.	office	huge	gun	similar	death
L.	score	forward	stretched	experience	allow
M.	located	workers	fear	Greek	led
N.	bought	women	march	northern	create
O.	British	difficult	match	doesn't	win
P.	steel	total	evening	determine	deal
Q.	details	rope	cotton	apple	none
R.	entire	corn	substances	smell	tools
S.	conditions	cows	track	arrived	seat
T.	Washington	division	effect	underline	view

book review

Teaching reading is both a science and art. Science and scientific studies have told us that phonics (word recognition) is essential to learning to read. The challenge for teachers is to teach this science to students in ways that are artful, creative, and engaging for students (and teachers).

Brian Kissman's *Phonics Things* is a superb example of how the science and art of teaching can complement one another. *Phonics Things* is a book that presents phonics concepts (letters and letter combinations, and the sounds they represent) through original paintings, poetry, and word play. Brian has been intentional in his development of *Phonics Things*. The illustrations, poetry, and word displays have been chosen to develop not only students' knowledge of phonics and its application in word recognition, but also to develop phonemic awareness, vocabulary, high level inferential comprehension, and aesthetic appreciation.

Phonics Things is a prime illustration of the way that phonics and reading can and should be taught—by informed teachers [and parents], using their wisdom and creativity to make something that has traditionally been taught in the most mundane ways (drill, repetition, worksheets, and rote memorization) into a learning activity that students will find incredibly engaging and satisfying—in both scientific and artistic terms.

Brian is an extraordinary teacher who has shown us how school, teaching, and learning can be for students and teachers.

Bravo!

Timothy Rasinski, Ph.D.
Professor Literacy Education
Kent State University
Kent, Ohio, USA